AND GOD SAID...

D1488517

AND GOD SAID...

A Brief History of Creation

Poems by

Barbara Leff

For Jason —
May God say only
wonderful things to you —

B

BROADSTONE BOOKS

God made everything out of nothing,
but the nothingness shows through.

PAUL VALERY (1871 - 1945)

Do you not see how necessary a world of pains
and troubles is to school an intelligence
and make it a soul?

JOHN KEATS (1795-1821)

CONTENTS

EPILOGUE

ACKNOWLEDGEMENTS

The following poems have appeared in these journals:

Journey (Eden Waters Press): 'Leaving the Garden'
Ibbetson Street: 'The Blessing'

Grateful acknowledgement to the many people whose support and encouragement have made this possible, including my dear friends and family, Debbie Aquaro, William Bell, Judy Blake, Stacey Siegel Bloom, Roger Berndt, Beth Randall Branigan, Sidney Brown, Lucy Cefalu, Joelle Chartier, Sheila Cohen, Ellen DiGiacomo; Joe Feringa, Ruth Gantman, Walter Gorman, Laurie Hall, Carl Hendrickson, Carole Jacoby, Raul Jacoby, Laura Kaplan, Martin Kravitz, Jack Patrick McGowan, Michael Meyers, Fran Miller, John Neitzel, Jody Patraka, Michael Reichman, Victoria Reichman, Lori Rubin, Paul Salisbury, Rachel Schochet, Wendy Schwartz, Marc Shapiro, Eileen Siegel, Gloria Siegel, Stephen L Simon, Karen Toloui, Deborah Udin, and M. J. Vineburgh.

Special thanks to Rabbi William Cutter, Mark Dowie, Alan Shapiro, Dr. Marleen Smith, Jane Anne Staw, Alicia Ostriker, and Sheila Potter for their careful reading and helpful comments; Rabbi Sheldon Marder for his rabbinical insights; Rabbi Eric Weiss for being an inspiration from the start; Jonathan Greene, David Maxim and Alan Siegel for their creative contributions; Kim Addonizio for the assignment that led to this book; Linda Kalinowski and Helen Luey for their moral support and belief in me; my dear friend and proof reader, Lynne Sherman; my publisher, Larry Moore, with whom it has been a pleasure to work; my eternal gratitude to Eloise Klein Healy for opening so many doors; and finally my partner, Arlene Singer for her steadfast support in everything.

PROLOGUE

A BRIEF HISTORY OF CREATION

*When God began to create heaven and earth, and the earth then
was welter and waste and darkness over the deep and
God's breath hovering over the waters…*

—Genesis 1:1-2

Before the beginning:
thought.
And thought begot word
and word became manifest:
darkness and light
land and sea
sun and moon,
according to plan.
And seeing that it was good
S/He said *root*
which grew into tree.
S/He said *beast*
and the sky took wing
the land slithered
and seas swam,
according to plan.
And seeing that it was good
S/He grew giddy
spurting words
for the sake of sounds:
plosives exploding
sibilants hissing.

And soon there was wo/man
seduced by serpent
which begot death.
And death begot time.
And seeing that it was late
S/he said *flood*
to make a clean start.
When that didn't work
S/He said *Messiah*
which begot war.
War begot holocaust.
And seeing what S/he had done
S/He said nothing
and sat back and waited.

AND GOD SAID...

MOONSHINE

And God said, 'Let there be lights in the vault of the heavens to divide the day from the night, and they shall be signs for the fixed times and for days and years, and they shall be lights in the vault of the heavens to light up the earth.' And so it was. And God made the two great lights, the great light for dominion of day' and the small light for dominion of night, and the stars.
— Genesis 1:14-17

So I told God
I would not – could not –
share dominion with the brassy braggart
who couldn't control his own eruptions.

God nodded in agreement
and I felt myself contract into a shadow
of my former self.

Then I told God
it was bad form
to punish me
for speaking the truth.

In response,
God promised
to extend my reign
into day.

So I told God
I would not – could not –
bask in another's glow,
my own light lost in his glare.

God promised
His people would count their seasons
according to my cycle

So I said
what of all the others
bound to number their days
by the comings and goings
of the fiery one?

God said humility
was the badge
of men of virtue
and holiness.

So I told God
I did not care
about the affairs
of men.

I said
He was skirting the issue,
side stepping my distress.

So God
waved His hand
and the sky shimmered
with a million crystals that stood still
save a few that danced
this way and that
disappearing
without a trace…

Distracted by the spectacle
my resolve waned
reducing my voice
to a whisper.

ADAM SPEAKS

And the Lord God cast a deep slumber on the human, and he
slept, and He took one of his ribs and closed over the flesh where
it had been, and the Lord God built the rib He had taken from
the human into a woman…
                    —Genesis 2:21-22

I woke with an ache
and a presence sleeping beside me,
bleating
like a dreaming dog.

I crawled to her.
She backed away.
I reached out.
She flinched.
I ventured my name.
She said nothing.

When I told her
she owed me her life,
I heard the telltale crack
of thunder.
I went on in a whisper
listing my wishes.

Lightning struck the tree
bequeathed to me,
sawed in half the limb
that had been
my shelter.

We clung to each other
beneath a canopy
of storm and fury
too scared to sleep,
falling into pre-dawn stupor
and clear skies.

Days passed quietly
and we forgot ourselves,
behaved as though the cosmos
were made for us.

As if among all creation
any man deserves more
than a peek at paradise.

LEAVING THE GARDEN

…and He brought her to the human…

—Genesis 2:22

When he blamed me
for the pain in his side
I said nothing.
When he blamed me
for sharing the light
I said nothing.
When he blamed me
for singing too loud,
for long walks alone,
befriending the others
and giving them names,
I said nothing.
I sought sleep's solace
in my favorite grove
and woke to a different voice-
sweet, sibilant-
murmuring my name
like a psalm.
The voice said *sorrow*
and I wept.
It said *longing*
and I heard something break.
It said *hunger*
and the earth rumbled around me
shaking loose
a fruit from the tree beside me.

I took a bite.
The green grove turned gold
and back again.
With another bite
I felt breeze on skin
I hadn't known
was naked.

After he consumed all
but the core,
he cursed me
as if I'd force fed him doubt.
Then he tattled.
Aware I'd take the fall,
I prepared to leave.
But the Big Voice,
sensing my intention,
went one step further,
and forced me
to take along the man.

THUS SPAKE THE SERPENT

Now the serpent was most cunning of all the beasts of the field that the Lord God had made. And he said to the woman, 'Though God said, you shall not eat from any tree of the garden–' And the woman said to the serpent, 'From the fruit of the garden's trees we may eat, but from the fruit of the tree in the midst of the garden God has said, "You shall not eat from it and you shall not touch it, lest you die."' And the serpent said to the woman, 'You shall not be doomed to die. For God knows that on the day you eat of it your eyes will be opened and you will become as gods knowing good and evil'.
— Genesis 3:1-6

Just another of the Old Man's creations
slinking along, thinking my own thoughts
when there began a terrible trembling.
The sky resounded
with a high-pitched squeal
and I slithered up the nearest tree.
When I witnessed the approach
of an ungainly she-creature
I knew I'd surely die.

I shrank into myself,
watched her eyes examine the tree
and come to rest upon me.
She bared her teeth
and I imagined her gorilla hands
in a death squeeze around my neck
and blurted nonsense
to save my scaly skin.

For this I earned
every epithet for evil
known to man.
The truth:
I didn't trick her into anything.

All I did
was ask a few leading questions
and take cues from her responses
till it was safe
to make my getaway.

FIRE

And on the eighth day
He sensed something missing,
sought solutions
for the flaws He noticed
once He'd stopped to rest.

Thus I was born
to be a messenger,
assuming my form
to talk to the chosen.
I roared into being,
and made the witness quake
in His presence.

He saw that it was good.
Without my consent
He turned me into a tool
to clear their land
and cook their food,
to keep them warm
and light their way.

So I raged out of control
until He made me the link
between heaven and earth,
bound by the laws of neither,
commanding the respect of all,
subject to His whims
and witness to His missteps.

16

CAIN'S CURSE

And the Lord set a mark upon Cain so that whoever found him would not slay him.
                    —Genesis 3:15

Yes I *was* marked,
stripped naked
desperate for anonymity.

First He cut the foreskin
but said it wasn't enough.
Then He etched a *vav* on my skull
but said it wasn't enough.

So He sheathed my hands
in so much silt
they hung from my sides
like barbells - dead weight
that itched and burned
at the slightest touch

Impossible to ignore
(harder still to hide)
I was branded:
The man with dirty hands.

Children sang of me
women swooned
and in a rare moment
of distraction
when I scratched my nose
the trail of blood
would bring me back.

HALF-BREED

The Nephilim were then on the earth, and afterward as well,
the sons of God having come to bed with the daughters of man
who bore them children: they are the heroes of yore,
the men of renown.

—Genesis 6:4

Mighty we were.
And doomed.
Dinosaurs–created to be destroyed.
Wafting in swirls of lavender and myrrh,
my father appeared to my mother in a dream.
He enveloped her
in great white wings.
Awakening, she felt herself conceive.
At my birth she turned from me,
then turned on Him.

You who have walked the earth for millennia
have the luxury to ponder the great questions.
Those of us issued from the union of spirit and substance
are born with the answer.
Woe unto you when you figure it out.

THE COVENANT

…and Jared begot Enoch…
       who begot Methuselah…
       who begot Lamech…
       who begot a son.
       And he called his name
       as Noah…
              —Genesis 5:18-29

A simple soul,
I was a comfort to my father.
A sower of seeds,
the earth itself
my closest companion.

He found me at dusk
as I surveyed the vines
snaking my name across the land.
I faltered, held fast to my staff.

All the accolades:
my own prudence
my wife's virtue,
the piety of my sons -
a con man's ploy.
He chose me
the way I reap my harvest:
at random.

And I fell for it
(as if I had a choice).
I didn't mind
His commandments
of this many cubits
and that many reptiles,
of this type of wood
and that type of pitch.
I didn't even mind
the stench that grew
into a living entity.

What bothers me
is the way He played me,
letting me release
bird after bird
when His all-along plan
was to open the ark
at His whim.

That . . .
and trashing the earth.
No mercy
for His own creation,
leaving me alone
to begin again.

AFTER THE DELUGE

And Noah, a man of the soil, was the first to plant a vineyard.
And he drank of the wine and became drunk, and exposed himself
within his tent. And Ham the father of Canaan saw his father's
nakedness and told his two brothers outside. And Shem and Japheth
took a cloak and put it over both their shoulders and walked back-
ward and covered their father's nakedness. And Noah woke from his
wine and he knew what his youngest son had done to him. And he
said, 'Cursed be Canaan, the lowliest slave shall he be to his brothers.'

—Genesis 9:20-25

Everyone loved me,
lavished me with figs and ditties,
saved me the sweetest meats,
the softest bed.

When my brothers
balked at doing my bidding,
a word from my father
set them straight.

And then the deluge…

Drifting, drifting,
I watched whole herds
steal pet names
once saved for me,
listened to my brothers
soothe swine with songs
once sung to me alone.

When I could take it
no more
I went to my father
found him tending
the vines he'd refused
to leave behind.
His speech slurred,
eyes at half mast
he muttered curses to himself,
laughed out loud.

When I returned the next night
I found him in the tent,
snoring and slobbering,
his body creased and mottled.
I gagged.

Regarding honoring one's father and mother.
I plead guilty before God.

Still
what honor is there
in a man
who would curse
his own grandchildren
for the deeds of his son?

AND GOD THOUGHT...

As the waters receded
and the earth emerged new-born
I said *never again.*
As the ark creaked open
and the creatures emerged,
bleating and squawking
and sniffing the scoured air,
I said *never again.*
As Noah and his flock
walked once more on the land,
I said *never again.*

In the hour of wrath
even as my tears drenched the world
and my bellowing caused great gales,
I said *never again.*
Even as I screamed,
I am that I am,
and I will not be disobeyed,
I said *never again.*
Even as I smote my own children
for asserting the free will I gave them
I said *never again,*
never again, never
again...

Where do I go
for forgiveness?
To whom may I turn
for redemption?

BREEDING EVIL

A fine irony.
Only one name among the many,
I gave rise to the nation
whose name became a synonym
for mass murder.
Both my father and his father
earned the same meager mention.

And the mothers? What of them?
Scripture suggests
all but a few Patriarchs sired their sons
from smoke and vapor.

Back before anyone
knew Gentile from Jew,
I tended the land my father granted me,
spoke to God when He called,
obeyed His word.

When so told, I took a wife,
brought forth three sons and two daughters,
whose names and histories,
like my wife's, were writ only on the wind.

I sent them forth to settle nations,
leaving me to live out my years alone.

With my last breath
I praised God for entrusting me
to re-populate His land,
for blessing me with sons so righteous
they needed little from me.

If I am at fault for what followed,
so be it.
Later ages may say it was God's will.

Still
it started with my seed.
And contrary to biblical precedent
despair so deep does not appear
out of thin air.

NIMROD

*And Cush begot Nimrod. He was the first mighty man on
earth. He was a mighty hunter before the Lord*
—Genesis 10: 8-9

Like all God's children,
I came into the world
clad in my own skin.
I do not recall my scent
as separate
from the animal skins
that covered me.

Like all God's children,
I was given a name.
Mine, *Mighty Hunter,*
foretold my future.

At 12, I walked the forest
in search of a spectral bird,
an offering to God,
found instead a herd of deer,
tried to hide behind a tree,
but not before a straggler buck
bowed down and let me take him
with my bare hands.

That night
after giving the remains to God
I had a dream.
Shorn of skins,
covered by deer hide dripping blood
that I alone could see,
its salty stench gagged me.

Years later
as I sat on my throne,
Babylon before me,
I saw something move,
shining like the sun.

Looking closer,
I saw the carcass
of a small deer,
which woke in my dreams
to devour me.

NIMROD 2

And they said, 'Come, let us build us a city and a tower with its top in the heavens, that we may make us a name, lest we be scattered over all the earth.'

—Genesis 11:4

Where's the divinity in submerging civilization?
And why start from scratch without reflection or remorse
just to reap the same result?

Was this the image
in which we were created?

We only wanted to build something with the hands he gave us,
the minds he fashioned for us.
We only wanted to realize the dominion
he'd bequeathed.

Long after we've returned to dust,
the creations of man will crowd the land,
towers the least of it.

If this god of ours
is forced to make a choice again,
may these words
come back to haunt him.

LOT IN LIFE

*And the Lord rained upon Sodom and upon Gomorrah
brimstone and fire from the Lord from the heavens. And
He overthrew all those cities and all the plain and all the
inhabitants of the cities and what grew in the soil. And
(Lot's) wife looked back and she became a pillar of salt.*

—Genesis 19:24-27

…if I'd chosen high ground,
    leaving the plains to Abram
if the wind hadn't sung woeful songs at dusk,
    nor whispered a ghost voice at dawn
if I'd planted crops, tended my cattle,
    remained with the land
if I'd not been blinded by city lights,
    stayed home and minded my own
if I'd read bedtime tales to the children
    and sometimes answered *yes*
if I'd heeded dreams of windblown wilderness,
    crashing boulders, flaming bodies
if I'd spent less time counting my shekels,
    shared more with the poor
if I'd not offered my virgin children
    to the wolves at the door
if I'd grasped my wife more tightly
if I'd kept her from looking back…

SALT

—Genesis 19:26-27

We were running
for our lives
the city behind us,
light sifting through clouds
marked the pre-dawn path.
When the wind warned me
to focus on the future
I thought I was dreaming,
tried to pinch myself awake
and felt not flesh
but grit between fingers
fading fast into memory.
I tried to scream
through a throat
clogged with sand,
tried to run on legs
that were no more.

With eyes destroyed
I watched the world speed by.
All discrete entities
merged together
then split apart
in circles of light,

concentric rings of color
consuming the objects
till all that remained
was a landscape of light
flashing past whatever
I'd become.

Being buried alive
is a slow road to hell,
but at least there's solace
in knowing it will end.

But woe unto she
who, buried alive,
beckons a death
that taunts her with silence
who prays for a sleep
that withholds its blessing
who begs forgiveness
for a sin she can't name
from a god who blows in
on a spectacle of light
leaving behind
a wake of salt
and whispers something
she can no longer hear.

UNHOLY UNION

And Lot came up from Zoar and settled in the high country,
his two daughters together with him, for he was afraid to dwell in
Zoar, and he dwelt in a certain cave, he and his two daughters.
And the elder said to the younger, 'Our father is old, and there is
no man on earth to come to bed with us like the way of all the
earth. Come, let us give our father wine to drink and let us lie
with him, so that we may keep alive seed from our father'…
And the two daughters of Lot conceived by their father.

—Genesis 19:30-36

1. *The Younger*

I was half asleep when she came to me
with a scheme so hare-brained
I thought I must be dreaming.

As the sharp edge
of reality pierced the fog
I kept my eyes shut
and willed her away.

This time, I told myself,
I'd hold my ground
refuse her demand
even as I knew she'd make me believe
black is white
down is up
bad is good.

Aswoon with wine,
my fantasy:
A stranger of tender touch
his seed the start of a new nation.

But after…
I felt my father's fetid breath on my face
his old man's fingers in my hair
his animal groans in the air.

Not my sister
who sang from her perch of pride
and waved me away
as if I were
no more than a speck of dust
or a dream of clouds
turning the noon sky gray.

2. *The Elder*

She thought I sought pleasure
as if lying with my father
could bring any joy.

She thought I sought her collusion
as if her consent
could ease my conscience.

She thought I sought a child
for my own comfort
as if caring for the old man
weren't burden enough.

I didn't tell her
about the plague of dreams
or the voices from the sky
or the visions flitting through the trees.

Day and night
two boys begging to be born
their eyes
like crystal reflecting light,
their cry
a clarion call
hailing a new nation.

Maybe God called,
maybe madness.
Once Moab was born
it ceased to matter which.

But sometimes
my son's eyes sparkle in a way
that makes me shudder
and I'm back in the cave,
with a faceless man
who was once
my father.

ON BEING A PROPHET

The astrologers stood aghast and whispered to
one another: 'Terah's son has just been born. He will be
a mighty Emperor. His descendants will multiply and
inherit the earth for all eternity, dethroning kings and
possessing their lands.'

—early ninth-century Midrash,
Pirkei de Rabbi Eliezer, chapter 26

I followed my father's ways
used hammer and chisel
to craft idols whose eyes saw nothing
whose lips spoke silence.

On my own
I tracked wayward stars
as they careened across the skies.

Once
I watched one reverse course
come right at me
stand still for an instant
and vanish.

The next day
as I held the hammer
above a half finished idol
its dead eyes set my hand atremble.
I smashed the head
that held those eyes.

Only later did I learn of the celestial spectacle
that took place on the night I was born.

And I knew
better than I've known anything
it was not my hand that shattered
the piece of clay,
not my will
that estranged me from my father,
not my choice to become
His servant
and certainly

Not within my power
to concoct the first Jew.

If asked
no doubt He'd tell you
it was written.

Whatever that means.

A MARRIAGE

And there was a famine in the land and Abram went down to Egypt to sojourn there, for the famine was grave in the land. And it happened as he drew near to the border of Egypt that he said to Sarai his wife, 'Look, I know you are a beautiful woman and so when the Egyptians see you and say, "She is his wife," they will kill me while you they will let live. Say, please, that you are my sister, so that it will go well with me on your count and I shall stay alive because of you.'

—Genesis 12:10-14

If truth be told
I agreed to the plan.
Possessed by hunger
I dreamt of olives and dates
and wells of water
only to awaken
with my mouth filled with sand.

He treated me like his sister.
How else explain his willingness
to hand me over to Pharaoh
like an offering?

If truth be told
it was an oasis flowing with water,
dates and figs falling from trees,
pillows so plush I slept without dream.

I missed him
rarely
showered as I was with gold and silk
from far-off lands.

I was happy there in the harem,
away from the world
and with God's help,
Pharaoh kept his distance.

When it came to an end
I cleaved to what he'd done
as if it were an infant,
nursed it with bile,
and when he tried again to humiliate me
in front of his whore Hagar,
I loosed my anger on him
till he sent her away.

If truth be told
I'll always wonder
if he agreed to sacrifice my son,
my only son,
to please God—
or to punish me.

THE BLESSING

*...And Abraham built there an altar and laid out the wood
and bound Isaac his son and placed him on the altar on top
of the wood. And Abraham reached out his hand and took
the cleaver to slaughter his son.*

—Genesis 22:9-11

When it was over,
when my father tilted his head
to better hear the demands of his delusions,
when he loosened my bindings
without a sigh or smile or some show of relief,
when he dismissed me with a wave
and ordered me to run and play like a good boy –
business as usual,
as if he had not just prepared
his only son for slaughter,

I crawled into a ball beneath the bushes
and covered my ears
to block out the bleating of the poor ram
who replaced me on the pyre,
became prey to bad dreams and fits of nausea,
found fear in alleys, well water, smiles.

When my father died
I spent three days sealing the tomb
to no avail.
His delusions found me
and ground what was left of me to a blind nub.

Now they call me a prophet
as they called my father,
as if delirium and bad dreams are a blessing.
If madness is a state of grace,
God must be the maddest one of all.

GOD LOOKS WITHIN

And the Lord's messenger called out to him from the
heavens and said, 'Abraham, Abraham!' and he said,
'Here I am.' and he said, 'Do not reach out your hand
against the lad and do nothing to him.'

—Genesis 22:11-12

I called him to the mountain
and told him to bind the boy.
No debate,
submission.
No justice,
blind faith.

And I?
I've anointed a man
who would speak out
for a city
yet offer his sons
without a sound.

GOING DOWN IN HISTORY

*And when her time was come to give birth, look, there
were twins in her womb. And the first one came out ruddy,
like a hairy mantle all over, and they called his name Esau.
Then his brother came out, his hand grasping Esau's heel,
and they called him Jacob.*

—Genesis 25:24-26

Jacob – *'He who supplants'*

I didn't know the color of my mother's eyes,
averted
the few times she spoke to me.

Favored by my father
I could bear the hairy face
that stared back
in dumb amazement
when I drank from oasis pools.

I didn't hear the words
my mother spoke to my brother
as they huddled
close enough to taunt me.

Blessed as I was by my father
I sang my song
to the creatures of the field.

I didn't value the books
my brother read,
his affected tone,
the shifty eyes
seeking soft spots
and shadows.

Blinded by the promise of birthright,
I climbed the highest peak
and shouted my joy
till my echo bounced back hollow
and I ran home
to find my mother and brother laughing
beside my sleeping father's tent.

With my mother looking straight at me
I saw myself through her eyes,
felt all that had been mine
fall from my shoulders
and cursed the womb
that had formed me.

My brother
reaping the bounty meant for me,
would live to tell a different tale.
Though I spoke the truth,
who'd look into this ragged face
and believe a single word?

MEASURE FOR MEASURE

And the children clashed together within her, and she said,
'Then why me?' and she went to inquire of the Lord. And
the Lord said to her, 'Two nations—in your womb, two
peoples from your loins shall issue. People over people
shall prevail, the elder, the younger's slave.'

—Genesis 25:22-23

In my mother's womb
her egg split
to form two selves struggling
for dominion.

While I appeared to comply with Esau
I grabbed hold of his heel
and we emerged as one.

The issue of birthright
was not cut and dried.
So the facts say
I deceived my father
into granting me his blessing.
Facts lie.

This world is a lie,
a metaphor for the truth
the senses conceal.

I walked the earth
believing my brother and I were separate.
I treated him as other.

The price I paid was steep:
years of exile to escape Esau's wrath –
marriage to the wrong sister –
seven years of toil –
to finally wed Rachel.

My brother's path was no less fraught
as I found when we came together
to bury our father.

How else could it be?

THE BOUT

And Jacob was left alone, and a man wrestled with him
until the break of dawn. And he saw that he had not won
out against him and he touched (Jacob's) hip-socket and
Jacob's hip-socket was wrenched as he wrestled with him
And (the man) said, 'Let me go, for dawn is breaking.'
And (Jacob) said, 'I will not let you go unless you bless me.'

—Genesis 32:25-27

I woke to nothing:
no sense of where
or who
or what I was
no memory of before
no inkling of next.

All was pain:
pulse in place of a heart
throbbing through me
as if my blood were on fire
and I saw
the specter of a hand
on my thigh
squeezing so hard
it lost all color.

(If it was a dream of Esau
seeking revenge
why the hairless hands?)

48

I heard the echo of my own voice
demanding to be blessed.
In reply
my opponent begged for release
in a tongue I'd never heard.

(How then did I know
his meaning?)

My arms ached
as if I'd borne my own body
on my back.

Now I stagger
from visions and voices
to solid sand and back again,
each step a study
in what it means
to be blessed.

WHAT'S IN A NAME

When morning came, look, she was Leah. And he said to
Laban, her father, 'What is this you have done to me?
Was it not for Rachel that I served you, and why have you
deceived me?'

—Genesis 29:25-26

Leah – *'Weary One'*

My name tells my story
Called *Weary* from birth
I was fated to face off with evil
I walked in my sister's shadow

Called *Weary* from birth
I was meant to marry Esau
I walked in my sister's shadow
So much for my birthright

I was meant to marry Esau
I ended up with Jacob
So much for my birthright
Jacob asked for my sister's hand

I ended up with Jacob
The greatest of deceivers
Jacob asked for my sister's hand
I took Rachel's place at the altar

The greatest of deceivers
Jacob met his match in me
I took Rachel's place at the altar
I bore him many sons

Jacob met his match in me
His piety a sham
I bore him many sons
My sister's womb was empty

His piety a sham
I saw his shadow self
My sister's womb was empty
Ravaged by bitter envy

I saw his shadow self
I was fated to face off with evil
Ravaged by bitter envy
My name tells my story.

THE BAKER

And the chief baker saw that he had solved well, and he
said to Joseph, 'I, too, in my dream—and look, there were
three openwork baskets on my head, and in the topmost
were all sorts of food for Pharaoh, baker's ware, and birds
were eating from the basket over my head.'…And Joseph
answered and said, 'This is its solution. The three baskets
are three days. Three days hence Pharaoh will lift up your
head from upon you and impale you on a pole and the
birds will eat your flesh from upon you.'

—Genesis 40:16-19

Not a dreamer by nature, I did as I was told,
toiled as a toddler for my father—
who foisted me off on Pharaoh for a good price—
and thanked the gods for the blessing
of work in the kitchen,
the shelter of a shed,
the soft bed I shared with mongrels
sniffing for edible scraps.
The reek of unwashed fur, the plague of tiny bites
that covered my body in a rapture of itching
were the price I paid for the warmth of their haunches.

I watched the crones knead and roll,
punch and pull dough as if trying to tame
a disobedient child or wayward spouse.
Soon my senses sang out
when unbaked bread became oven-ready
and my wares were deemed the best in the land.

Had I known Pharaoh's rage
would rise along with my fame,
I doubt I'd have done anything different,
even now knowing I'd end up in the dungeon,
drier and less drafty than my shed.

I only regret allowing Joseph to explain my dreams.
At first it was a silly game
believing baskets of bread picked at by birds
would foretell my beheading.

Now I stand beneath the branch that will bear me,
as vultures swoop and crowds gather.
In the minutes left to me, it's not Pharaoh I fault,
but Joseph.

We all know we're going to die.
But knowing the how and when
thrashes the soul like stone-ground wheat,
leaving barely a husk to hang in the wind.

PHAROAH DENOUNCES HIS GOD

…and Pharaoh said to Joseph, 'I have dreamed a dream
and none can solve it, and I have heard about you that you
can understand a dream to solve it.'

—Genesis 41:15-16

Like my father and his fathers
I was formed in the womb of divinity
brought forth with Re's own hand
and suckled on the milk of might.

Like my father and his fathers
I came of age, panned for gold.
But finding only coal
I kept my failings to myself
for the sake of kingdom and crown.

Three times I prayed to Re
and three times
a rainbow spread across my vision
so bright its halo flickered for days.

When Joseph appeared
wrapped in a rainbow
I bowed down,
believing Re had sent son and savior.
I gave the stranger dominion
over all the land.

As Joseph prophesized,
the trees bore fruit
so plump it fell from branches,
the beasts of the fields
grew bellies and haunches
like children spoiled
on the fat of the land.

Amid rumors of roads
strewn with bones and teeth
I asked Re to smile on my success
but he answered with visions
of sandstorms and skeletons,
howling winds and wretched cries.
I considered turning to Joseph's god
then realized He'd already bestowed
the blessings I begged of Re:
praise from my people,
my might taken to its limit.

THE DEATH OF JOSEPH

And Joseph said to his brothers, 'I am about to die, and
God will surely single you out and take you up from this
land to the land He promised to Isaac and Jacob.'

—Genesis 50:24-25

By the time his brothers assembled,
Joseph's skin had turned translucent,
features fading into a fine light
as he foretold the terms
of the Exodus.

Levi
squinting into the glare
that consumed his brother
broke down seeing Joseph's mouth sag.
Even as his voice filled the room
Joseph's eyes continued to regard him
through lids made of glass.

In the silence
that followed Joseph's final wish –
that his bones be brought to the Promised Land –
Reuben felt a flutter at his ear,
heard the whisper of his name
and shivered in a final
flash of light.

For the rest of his life
the slightest breeze
would bring him back
to the flash of light
his whispered name
the split-second stroll with Joseph
in a sun-strewn garden
as if his return to the present
was punishment
for selling his own blood
into slavery.

AND BY MY NAMES SHALL YE KNOW ME

*And Moses said to God, 'Look, when I come to the
Israelites and say to them, "The God of your fathers has
sent me to you," and they say to me, "What is His name?"
what shall I say to them?'*

—Exodus 3:13-14

In the beginning was My name
and My name was *YHWH*
but *YHWH* was ineffable
so they called Me *HaShem*,
'The Name,' which was not a name
so they called Me *El*
which fell far short of meaning
so they called Me *Elohim*
which plurified both My name
and their reasons for retreat
so they called Me *Adonai*,
'My Lord,' which worked for a while
until Abraham twisted *Shaddai*
to mean 'He Who Destroys.'
His son's son restored it
to its rightful meaning 'Almighty'
which pleased Me until Moses recoiled
and I claimed the name
Ehyeh-Asher-Ehyeh,
'I AM THAT I AM'
YHWH in human-speak.

Let them call Me what they will.
My name is known to Me alone
lest it land on the wrong lips.
Then Heaven help us all.

EPILOGUE

ENDGAME

In the end God can no longer bear
the bickering and back stabbing,
the whimpers and whines
that ooze from the cauldron of Earth
and poison the skies,
punch holes in the heavens.

S/He grows weary of men's ploys and pretexts—
greenhouse gases and *global warming*—
as if by fixing a name, a category, a syndrome
to the mess of their own making
they can file it away and wait
for the rapture, the first or second coming,
satori, nirvana, the virgins at the gate.

S/He can no longer bear to hear the cries
of dying breeds of creatures
gasping in the human miasma of *me, me, me,*
the bleeding of angels, their pleas for refuge
from the pendulum swing of hope, despair
and back again.

And yet God
Who set the whole thing in motion
struggles against fixing a name, a category,
a syndrome to this creation,
spinning it out of site
and beginning the next project.

So S/He sits on the precipice
continues the multi-millennial vigil
above the patchwork planet
and sees the landscape
not as a quiet quilt
but as a chess board—
pawns, rooks, queen and king
invisible in the vastness of space,
their time on Earth
not even a nanosecond.

God weighs the options:
to tumble the board like a sore loser
or to play for keeps.

NOTES

Page 7, MOONSHINE

According to ancient scholars, at the time of the Creation the moon
was of the same size as the sun. The moon then objected that it
would not be decorous for two kings to use one crown, whereupon
God diminished her size. In reply to the moon's question, 'Ought I
to be punished for having spoken reasonable words?'

Page 17, CAIN'S CURSE

Some Jewish teachings state that Cain became white – a leper. This
made people avoid him. Some sources believe that a horn grew out
of Cain's forehead in order to protect him. Others believe that God
engraved a letter of His name on Cain's forehead to warn people not
to kill him. And others believe God gave him a protective dog.
—Midrash Aggadah 4:15, Bereishet Rabbah 22:28, Tiffert Tziyon

Page 19, HALF-BREED

The sons of God. In Hebrew *Benei Elohim* describes angels, demi-
gods or other divine messengers. Many rabbinical scholars believe
this is a reference to early pagan mythology.

Page 22, AFTER THE DELUGE

In the fifth commandment, Honor thy father and thy mother, the
word honor originally referred only to the adult child attending to
the physical needs of the elderly parents. It has since come to refer
as well to treating one's parents with respect and reverence.

Page 28, NIMROD

According to the Talmud, Nimrod's great success in hunting was due
to the fact that he wore the coat of animal skins which God made for
Adam and Eve.

Page 37, ON BEING A PROPHET

Pirke De-Rabbi Eliezer (*Chapters of Rabbi Eliezar*) is an interpretive
work on *Genesis,* part of *Exodus,* and a few sentences of *Numbers,* as-
cribed to R. Eliezer ben Hyrcanus (80-118 C.E.).

Page 41, THE BLESSING

When Abram was ninety-nine, God came to him and told him he
would no longer be called Abram; instead he would be called Abra-
ham, father of a multitude.

Page 63, ENDGAME

In Jewish thought, the Messiah is believed to be a human leader who
ushers an era of peace into the world.

ABOUT THE AUTHOR

Born and raised in New York, Barbara Leff discovered poetry at the age of 12, and has explored the genre ever since. Co-founder of the Caselli Street Poets, her work has appeared in numerous journals, including *Faultline, Fourteen Hills,* and *Ibbetson Street.* She lives in San Francisco with her partner and brood of four-legged furry ones. *And God Said…* is her first collection.